GETTING A JOB IN
CHILD CARE

ANASTASIA SUEN

ROSEN
PUBLISHING®

NEW YORK

Published in 2014 by The Rosen Publishing Group, Inc.
29 East 21st Street, New York, NY 10010

First Edition

Library of Congress Cataloging-in-Publication Data

Suen, Anastasia.
Getting a job in child care/by Anastasia Suen.—1st ed.—New York: Rosen, c2014
    p. cm.—(Job basics: getting the job you need)
Includes bibliographical references and index.
ISBN 978-1-4488-9612-7
1. Child care—Vocational guidance—Juvenile literature. 2. Child care—
Vocational guidance—United States—Juvenile literature. I. Title.
HQ778.5 S84 2014
649.023'73

Manufactured in the United States of America

CPSIA Compliance Information: Batch #S13YA: For further information, contact Rosen Publishing, New York, New York, at 1-800-237-9932.

CONTENTS

INTRODUCTION

Parents everywhere need child care. What that looks like is different for each family. Jennifer takes her baby to a family home every morning on her way to work. The mother in this home has her own small children. She can take care of one or two more without a license from the state.

Linda takes her one-year-old child to a family home each morning. The six children who go to this licensed child care center don't live there. They play in a child care room made just for them. There is also play equipment for them in the backyard.

Brittany's two young children arrive at a larger family child care center at 6:30 AM. Two women care for sixteen children during the day. Brittany's two-year-old stays at the center all day. After Brittany's six-year-old eats breakfast, she goes to the elementary school across the street. A day care worker takes her to school in the morning and picks her up in the afternoon.

Tamika and her five-year-old "go to work" together in the morning and come home together at night. While Tamika works at the hospital, her son is learning his letters at the employee child care center.

Lauren often travels for work, so she has a nanny for her two children. The nanny lives with the family and works six

Sarah Simanskey runs a family child care center in her home. Here, she reads to her two-year-old son and two other young children in her care.

days a week. Lauren's nanny drives the children to school in her own car. The nanny also shops for the family and prepares all of the meals.

Jennifer takes her two children to elementary school in the morning on her way to work. At the end of the school day, they go to the school gym for after-school care. Jennifer's children eat snacks and play games. They also do their homework before she picks them up at 6:30 PM.

There are a lot of child care options for parents. All of those options need trained child care workers. Will you watch children in a home day care or work as an assistant in a family child care center?

Maybe you can live with a family and be a nanny or a manny (a male nanny). You won't have to pay rent while you are there. That will cut down on your expenses.

A job in a child care center may be right choice for you. You will work with children and other adults in a structured setting.

There are child care jobs out there waiting for you. Before you start, let's see what the job is like day to day. We'll explore what kind of training you'll need. The good news is you can start getting ready for work right now, even if you are still in high school.

Practical steps come next. We'll talk about how to find a job listing and what to add to your résumé. Then we'll cover the all-important interview. What will they ask you, and what will you ask them? (Yes, you have to interview your employer, too.)

After you are hired, there is still more to do. You need to bring in your paperwork and fill out even more. Taxes, health insurance, and continued training are all necessary. You don't need a college degree to work in child care, but you do need to keep training to keep your job. The good news is, now your employer can pay for it!

Child Care Today

When you work in a child care job, you are responsible for taking care of children. You fill in for the parents while they go to work. Becoming a surrogate parent is really your job. What will you do during the day? Let's look at a chart from the Bureau of Labor Statistics' *Occupational Outlook Handbook* listing for child care workers.

Child care workers typically do the following:
- Supervise and monitor the safety of children in their care
- Prepare meals and organize mealtimes and snacks for children
- Help children keep good hygiene
- Change the diapers of infants and toddlers
- Organize activities so that children can learn about the world and explore interests
- Develop schedules and routines to ensure that children have enough physical activity, rest, and playtime
- Watch for signs of emotional or developmental problems in children and bring the problems to the attention of parents
- Keep records of children's progress, routines, and interest

In a family child care center, the children eat and play just like they do at home. These children are eating their snacks in their play kitchen.

A parent does all of this every day, and so will you. The biggest difference is that you must also report all of this to the child's parents. You will need to keep a log of what each child does throughout the day. For infants, this means that every bottle given and every diaper changed is written in the log. If a child falls while learning how to stand, that is recorded, too. So is the first time the child can stand by himself or herself. Everything the child does during the day is written in the log for the parents.

Where the Jobs Are

So many parents today work, and someone needs to take care of all the children. That opens job possibilities for you. Let's look at the last census and see where the jobs are.

Every ten years the country takes a census. It's like taking roll in school. Names and ages are written down house by house across the country. The type of job each person has is also included. (On the 2010 census, your "job" was probably listed as "student.")

In 2010, there were more than 1.3 million jobs in child care. Let's drill a little deeper and see where those jobs were.

Bureau of Labor Statistics 2010 Child Care Workers Job Chart:

Child day care services: 22%
Private households: 15%
Elementary and secondary schools: 11%
Religious, grantmaking, civic, professional, and similar organizations: 8%

Choices

The good news for you is that there are a lot of choices. And those choices will continue to grow. The Bureau of

Every summer, teens work as counselors at summer camps all around the country. They work outside and serve as role models for younger kids.

Labor Statistics says that "employment of child care workers is expected to grow by 20 percent from 2010 to 2020, faster than the average for all occupations."

Where do you want to start? Do you want to work with a group of children that are the same age? Then a job in a child care center is the best fit for you. In the larger centers, the children who are the same age are placed in groups. This may also be the case at large after-school and summer programs. School-age children are often grouped together by their ages.

In a smaller child care center, you will probably find groups with a wider age range. This is how many family child care centers work, too. Locations that allow members to come at any time, like the gym or a hotel, also have a wide range of ages. If you like to work with several different ages at once, these smaller centers may be the best choice for you.

When you work as a nanny, you are working with only one family at a time. You will see other children and other nannies when you go out to the park. If

USE YOUR PHONE

If you work as a nanny, you can use your smartphone instead of a written log. Taking photos and sending text messages throughout the day will keep the parents up on their child's latest activities and accomplishments. You have your phone with you at all times anyway, so why not use it?

Technology can help you do your job. Use your phone to keep in touch with the child's parents throughout the day. They would take photos if they were there. Now it's your job.

you want to live where you work, a nanny position may be the right choice for you.

The place you want to work in the first choice you have to make. The second choice is the age of the children. Caring for an infant is very different than caring for a five-year-old. What you need to do for a child changes with age. Each stage has its plusses and minuses. What age do you enjoy the most? Do you enjoy rocking babies or pushing swings for preschoolers, or would you rather help out with homework after school?

There isn't a right or wrong answer. Parents get to enjoy all of the stages. Over time you can enjoy them all, too. The question is where do you want to begin?

How to Prepare for a Job in Child Care

I n most places, only a high school diploma is required to work in child care. While you are in high school, you can take classes that can help you get ready for your new job working with children.

Classes to Take in High School

Something you can do now is to take a child development class at your high school. This is the best way to start getting ready for a job in child care. The more you know about how children change as they grow up, the better. Nurturing a child's development is a major part of any child care job.

Taking child development classes in high school can also help you get a job in child care. It shows an employer that you have some training. That might make the difference between getting hired or not.

If your high school also has a preschool on campus, you might be asked to work there for some of your class assignments. At some schools the preschool is called the child development laboratory. Just like you do in the lab for your science classes, you would work in the child development lab to learn new things.

The lessons you learn in your child development class will help you understand how preschool children think and move. Taking that knowledge and using it with real children will move you to the next step. You will see these child development stages in action.

If you have the opportunity to work in a child development laboratory, you will be guided by the teachers who work there. At first, you will be asked simply to observe the teacher working with children. Now that you know more about child development, you can see why the teacher does what he or she does. How do the children react to him or her? Do they respond the way the child development lessons said they would?

After you have observed the preschoolers in action, the next step is for you to interact with the children yourself. The teachers in the lab will help you prepare to work with the preschool students. One of the teachers will meet with you before and after you work with the preschoolers. That teacher will help you plan what to do and then watch you do it. The preschool teacher will supervise you.

After you work with the children, the preschool teacher will talk with you about what worked and what didn't. Some ideas sound great when you write them down, but they just don't work in the classroom. Figuring out why they didn't work helps you grow as a child care worker. (It can also help your grade in the class.) Was it the way you explained things to the children, or was the task simply not appropriate for this age? Or could it be that it just wasn't right for this group of children? Not every child learns the same way.

After you talk about what worked and what didn't, you can make plans for the next lesson or the next day. This is what full-time child care workers do, too. At the end of the day, there is always a new day to plan. The child development laboratory teacher can help you make those plans. You can put your new ideas to work the next time you work with the

Working with young children as part of your classwork will give you valuable work experience. It will also give you a taste of your future job in child care.

children. This day-after-day work with children during high school will give you valuable work experience in child care.

Most child development programs discuss the child from birth to age eight. That's important, but that's not all there is for you to learn. Colleges with child development programs recommend that you take psychology and nutrition classes in high school. If your school offers a class in family relations, add this to your list. When you work with young children, you will also be working with their families. Working with parents will be an important part of your job every day.

Safety Training

Another thing you can do right now is to complete your safety training. Safety is always a concern for those who work with children. Young children often do not know the safety rules, nor do they know how to keep themselves healthy. As a child care worker, you would be responsible for the health and safety of the children in your care.

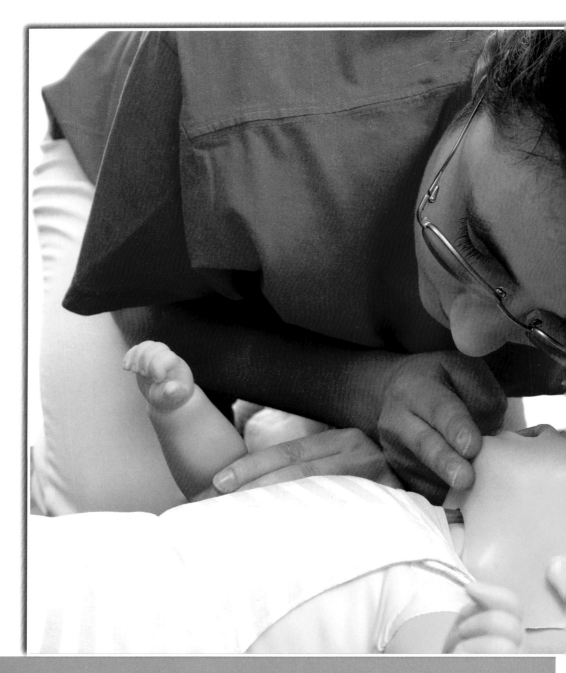

Taking a class at the Red Cross can help you save a child's life. In the class you will practice with an infant dummy. This doll can help you save a real life.

You can take the two safety classes you need right now. Take first aid and CPR (cardio-pulmonary resuscitation) at the Red Cross. You will need to take both of these classes to work at any child care job, so do it now.

Training in CPR can help you save someone's life if a person stops breathing or his or her heart stops beating. Performing CPR on an infant or child is not the same as CPR for a full-sized adult. You will learn the life-saving techniques you need to use for children in the CPR child and infant class.

First-aid classes will show you how to handle minor medical emergencies like cuts, burns, and insect bites. You will also find out what to do with sudden illnesses as well as head, neck, and back injuries. Because child care takes place year round, heat and cold emergencies will also be covered.

Children and Heatstroke

The National Highway Traffic Safety Administration says that "heatstroke is the leading cause of non-crash, vehicle related deaths for children under the age of 14." It happens two different ways. Children climb into cars and can't get back out. Or a child falls asleep during a drive and the adult forgets that the child is in the vehicle. It happens with day care vans and family cars.

HEAD START

Did you know that the federal government is in the child care business? All over the country there are Head Start programs. This federal program is for children from birth to age five and their parents. Head Start provides services for low-income families in every state. In most communities, Head Start is a preschool program for three- to five-year-olds.

Many Head Start programs also have an Early Head Start program. This program starts before a child is born. Early Head Start works with pregnant women who have incomes below the federal poverty level. After the women give birth, the program continues to work with their families as the infants grow into toddlers.

You may be able to find a job in a Head Start program near you. Head Start staff members work in centers or schools. They also visit homes.

Head Start is working to educate young families, so it wants its staff to keep learning, too. As of 2013, workers in Head Start programs must be enrolled in a training program. They must be working to earn an associate's degree in early childhood education or a child development credential.

It takes only a few minutes for the heat inside a car to rise. The Louisiana State Medical Society tested cars with the windows open and the windows closed. Opening the windows does not make the car cooler. The temperature inside both cars rose to 125 degrees Fahrenheit (52 degrees Celsius) in twenty minutes. In forty minutes, it was almost 140 degrees (60 degrees Celsius). The quick rise in temperature can cause death, brain injury, blindness, or hearing loss.

In addition to CPR and first aid, you will also need training in how to give medication to children in child day care. For example, if you live in New York, the state requires that all child care workers have medication administration training (MAT). To keep working, you need to renew your MAT certification every three years. You can take a face-to-face class or study online.

Certification

Although you do not have to have a college degree to work in child care, you do have to be working toward a certificate. In the United States, there are two child care certificate programs. The most common one is the Child Development Associate (CDA) certification awarded by the Council for Professional Recognition. The other program you will hear about is the Child Care Professional (CCP) designation offered by the National Child Care Association. Both of these certificates are awarded after on-the-job work experience and classwork. You will work on these certificates while you are employed.

To earn a CDA, you must have a high school diploma, 480 hours of child care experience, and 120 hours of formal training. To show that you have met these requirements, you need paperwork from both your employer and the school you are attending. You also need to be observed while you are working with young children.

If you are a junior or a senior in an early childhood education (ECE) program at your high school, you can start working on your CDA now. The child development classes you take at school and the work you do in the child development laboratory will count for your certificate. Ask your child development teacher to help you document your work.

Some high school child development classes use a computerized doll. The doll acts just like a real baby. It doesn't stop crying until you take care of it.

Where you work with children will determine what type of CDA you earn. There are CDAs for family child care programs, home visitor programs, and center-based programs. All of these certificates cover working with children from birth to age five. If you work in a center, however, there is even more specialization. You can earn an Infant/Toddler CDA (birth to thirty-six months) or Preschool CDA (ages three to five).

A CCP certificate is for early childhood teachers who do not have another degree. There are eleven requirements for this one, including 720 hours of child care work and 180 clock hours of training. After you earn this certificate, you must renew it with twenty new clock hours of training every two years.

An Associate's Degree in Early Childhood Education

Another way to train for your job is to attend classes at the local community college. Many community colleges allow you to start taking classes before you graduate from high school. You will need a high school transcript and proof of residence to enroll. Your state test scores will also be needed. The college may ask you to take reading, writing, and math tests, too. These test results will determine which reading, writing, and math classes you take for your degree.

At some high schools, you can earn double credit for any college classes that you take. A college class will count as both a high school class and a college class. Ask your guidance counselor what the rules are at your school.

How much your college tuition costs is based on where you live. Local students who live in the same city or county as the college will pay the lowest costs. Whatever the cost is, you can still apply for scholarships or grants to help you pay for your schooling. If you ask for a student loan, you will have to pay the money back later, with interest added. A scholarship or grant does not need to be repaid.

It will take you two years to earn an associate's degree if you

Taking child development classes now can help you get a job in child care later. You can take classes at your high school or at a nearby college.

go to school full-time. That means taking four or five classes a semester for two years. Not everyone goes to community college full-time, so you can take a few classes now. After you get a job, you can continue your studies at night or on the weekends. (Yes, some colleges offer Saturday classes.) Taking one class a semester during your senior year and one summer class will allow you to complete three classes. That's half of the first semester of college completed.

As you study for your associate's degree, you will take two types of classes. Everyone working toward a degree must take general education classes, like English composition or math. You will also take classes like child guidance or creative arts for early childhood for your early childhood development major.

After you complete your two-year degree, you may decide to transfer your credits to a four-year university. If you want to be a director someday, this may be the right choice for you. To work in administration, you need a college degree.

How to Find a Job in Child Care

How can you find a job in child care? Use your networks. Go online and look at job Web sites. Ask your school counselor. Talk to your family and friends.

Spread the word far and wide. Tell everyone you know that you are looking for work. Someone that you know may know someone who can hire you. People can't help you if you don't ask.

Your Résumé

Before you start filling out online job applications, take the time to create a one-page résumé. A résumé will highlight the key points you want an employer to remember. It will also help you remember what to write each time you fill out a job application.

Your name, address, and phone number go in the header. Use a bold or larger font so that it stands out. If you include an e-mail address, make sure that it has your real name in it, not a fun nickname.

This is also a good time for you to update the message on your phone from fun to professional. You don't want the employer to think she called the wrong number. Use your name in the message and promise to call back. That will let the employer know she has reached you.

Under your name you will need five headings. Write the name of each header in bold letters. Add an extra space between each section, too.

The first header should say "Objective." After that, list your objective. Use something that matches the description of the job you are applying. For example: "Seeking an entry-level position [in a home day care/day care center/as a nanny] where I can use my child care skills and abilities."

The second header is "Skills." Under this, make a bullet-point list of the child care skills you have. Write five to seven short phrases like, "Able to involve children in playing and learning activities" or "Caring and creative." List your CPR and first-aid certifications here.

The next header is "Work Experience." This is where you list the work you have already done: the babysitting,

Making a one-page résumé is the best place to start. This summary of your skills and education can help you get the job you want.

the day care at church, the work in the child development laboratory at your high school, etc.

For the "Education" header, you can write the name of your high school and the year you will (or did) graduate.

The final header is "References." Most people write just three words: "Available upon request." This means you have asked three adults to recommend you and your work to any employer who calls them. The best references know you well and have seen you work at the type of job you are applying for. Ask your child development teacher and your babysitting parents.

Save a copy of your résumé as a document and a PDF. (You can find a free PDF converter online that will change your document to a PDF.) Some employers will want you to bring a résumé with you to a job interview. Others will ask for it before they meet with you. You can attach your résumé to an e-mail or an online job application.

Your Job Application

What you write on an application is very important. Take your time so that you can make a good impression. Read the entire form before you fill it. Then use your résumé to look up all of the addresses and dates you need to fill out it out completely. Don't leave anything blank. If a question does not apply to you, write N/A for "Not Applicable" so that the employer knows that you didn't skip that line.

If you are filling out the form online, make a copy of it before you press send. Look it over for any mistakes. Correct any errors and print another copy. Now you are ready to submit it and apply for the job.

USE THE PUBLIC LIBRARY

If you don't have Internet access at home, you may be able to use the free computers at your public library. All you need is a library card. Use your ID to sign up for one. Then log on to a computer and start searching.

If you type "child care jobs" into a search engine, you'll see thousands of listings. Start with a job search engine instead. It looks for new job listings on company Web sites, in newspapers, and on job boards. Job search engines also let you compare salaries by job types and locations.

Job search engines are very simple to use. Just enter the type of job you're looking for and the location and check out the results.

There are also job search engines just for caregivers that will allow you to look for a child care job in your area. You can also create your own listing so that families can find you. Use the rate calculator to see what other caregivers in your area charge.

For applications that you fill out in person, always take two copies of the form. Use one as your practice copy. Bring an erasable pen so that you can correct any errors. Then fill out the second copy with neat handwriting. They can't hire you if they can't read your writing.

Write the name of the company and the date you applied on the practice copy. Save it so that you remember where you applied and what you wrote. Most job applications ask the same questions, so you can use old ones to help you fill out the new ones.

Do your homework before you contact any potential employers. Go online to find out what the jobs in your area pay. The more you know ahead of time, the better.

Salary

What type of salary can you expect? It depends on the type of job you have. It also depends on where you live. Go to a jobs Web site and search for child care jobs. Often, the salary will be listed. Most child care jobs will pay above minimum wage. The minimum wage is the lowest wage, or pay, you should get. This amount is set by law.

The minimum wage in each state is not the same. The U.S. Department of Labor has a minimum wage chart online. It lists the minimum wage for each state and U.S. territory. So what will you get paid? The U.S. Department of Labor says that where there are two different minimum rates, the highest one should apply.

What it costs to buy the things you need every day is always changing. Ten of the fifty states have laws that link the minimum wage to the consumer price index. That's a huge list of the prices that consumers pay to buy things.

The government keeps track of what it costs to buy things in over two hundred categories. Each month it records the prices of about eighty thousand items. This includes food, clothing, housing, transportation, medical care, recreation, education, and other personal expenses.

Once you start working, you will be paying for all of these things, too. You will have your own consumer price index. Another name for this is a budget. What does it cost you to buy the things you need each month? Do the math now and figure out what you need to make each month to pay your bills.

Asking for Help

Your high school counselor may be able to help you find a job. There are also workshops that help you search and apply for a job. Some churches offer these workshops. Your state employment office may also train you. Some states offer these workshops for a small fee or free of charge.

You can also find job searching help online. Most job search engines have advice pages. The state of Nevada has a Web site just for young people looking for work.

A Nanny Agency

If you want to work as a nanny, it might be easier to work with an agency. The nanny agency's job is to find nannies for local families. The agency will interview you and make sure that you have all of the paperwork and training that you need. It will also do a background check on you. Agencies do not get paid until they find you a job, so they are very motivated to work for you. You don't pay the agency any money. The family that hires you will pay the agency a fee for finding you.

To sign up for an online nanny agency listing, you just have to fill out the application. Once you are registered on the nanny Web site, families who are interested in you can contact you. These agencies make money by charging the parents a fee for signing up. Some also charge a fee for processing all of the paperwork.

Licenses

Most states require child care centers and home day care centers to have a license. This means you must pass a background check to work there. The state does not want people with a criminal record working with young children. The safety of the children is very important.

Another safety item is your health. To work in child care, you must show an employer your immunization records. You also need these records to attend school, so ask your parents for them.

Most state licenses require that workers have child care training. This is why it is so important to take child development classes in high school. Your first-aid and CPR classes count.

Job Fairs

A job fair is a quick way to meet a lot of employers all at once. At a job fair, employers from several companies set up tables and talk to potential employees. You can fill out your application and give the employer a copy of your résumé.

Before you meet with an employer or visit a job fair, ask a friend to interview you. Talking out your answers ahead of time will help you.

Job fairs for child care jobs are often combined with "teacher career" job fairs. They usually take place at a community center. These employers are all looking for someone to hire, so dress just as you would for a job interview.

Networking

Someone you already know may be able to help you get a job. Tell everyone you know that you are looking for a job in child care. Tell your friends and your family. Tell the people you know in your neighborhood, your church, and your clubs at school. There is always a need for child care workers. Let the people you know spread the word and help you find a job.

CHAPTER FOUR

The Job Interview

Most employers have more people apply for a job than they can hire. Your job application is your first "job interview." Employers use the job application to screen potential employees. Most job applicants do not hear back after this step. If the employer does not want to hire you, they will not contact you.

If an employer thinks that you might be a good match, you will be asked for an interview. Some companies will interview you more than once. They may want to interview you over the phone first. Then they will call you in for a face-to-face interview. At some companies you will interview with two or three people (all together or one at a time).

Practice Makes Perfect

Before you have your first interview, think about what you would say to a potential employer. Ask a friend to "interview" you by asking these common child care interview questions.

1. Why did you apply for this position?
2. Why should we choose you for this position?
3. What kind of experience do you have working with children?
4. How do you handle discipline?
5. How would you handle conflict with parents?

During an interview, a friendly smile and positive attitude go a long way toward helping an employer decide how you would act as an employee.

6. What do you want children in your care to learn?

7. What are your strengths and weaknesses?

Practicing your answers beforehand will help you on the day of your interview. Because you have practiced ahead of time, you will already know your answers. That will make you look confident and experienced, and these are both traits that employers want.

Phone Interviews

Some busy employers, including families that want nannies, will want to talk to you on the phone first. A phone interview is an easy way to screen a large number of job applicants. In other words, employers use phone interviews to eliminate some of the job applicants.

To stay in the running, act just like you would if you were meeting with the employer in person. Give the caller your full attention by taking the call in a quiet room. Don't take the call while you are in the car or on a takeout line.

Make sure that you smile when you are being interviewed over the phone. Your positive emotions and friendly tone will reveal themselves in your voice.

Don't interrupt the call to do something else. During a phone interview, talking to that employer is the most important thing you can do.

Remember to smile as you talk. Your caller can't see you, but your emotions can be heard in your voice. You want the employer to know that you feel positive about yourself and the job.

Face-to-Face Interviews

If you pass the phone interview step, you will be asked to come in for a face-to-face interview. Now you will be judged by what you say and how you act and what you wear.

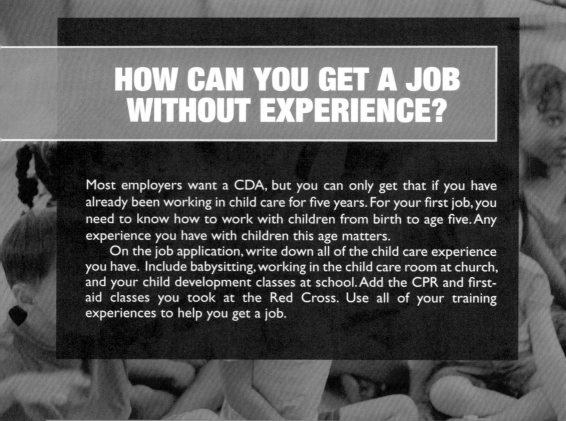

HOW CAN YOU GET A JOB WITHOUT EXPERIENCE?

Most employers want a CDA, but you can only get that if you have already been working in child care for five years. For your first job, you need to know how to work with children from birth to age five. Any experience you have with children this age matters.

On the job application, write down all of the child care experience you have. Include babysitting, working in the child care room at church, and your child development classes at school. Add the CPR and first-aid classes you took at the Red Cross. Use all of your training experiences to help you get a job.

What to Wear

To get a job, you need to dress the part. That means you need to look like you already work there. The clothing that you wear to work is not the same as clothing you wear for school or for home. You will need to cover your tattoos and skip the perfume. (You don't want to lose a job because your potential employer is allergic.) You will also need to leave most of your jewelry at home. You don't want an employer to remind you that little children pull dangly earrings and necklaces. Only wear "child-safe" jewelry to a job interview.

Make a Test Run

You don't want to be late for a chance at a paying job, so take a test drive the day before. Go online and make a map from home to work. Then test it out and see how long it takes to get there. If you are taking public transportation, you will need to add walking time. If you are driving, you'll need to add time to find a place to park.

Once you know how long it takes to get there, add a few minutes. Plan to arrive a few minutes early the following day. You need time to walk into the building and find the meeting room, too.

On the Day of the Interview

Today is the day! After a good night's sleep, wake up and have breakfast. Take a shower and wash your hair, too. Then get dressed as if you were going to work.

On the day of the interview, dress the part. That means getting dressed as if you were already working there. If you want to be treated like an adult, you need to dress like one.

Put your résumé in your bag and get on the road. You want to arrive early so that you have time to observe the other workers.

When you get there, go inside and introduce yourself. Stand and smile, and greet the interviewer by name. Shake his or her hand with a firm grip and keep eye contact. Breathe and stay relaxed, confident, and friendly.

After you go to the interview room, remember to sit up straight. Be polite and ask questions as well as answer them. Be honest but also positive about yourself.

Child Care Center Interviews

At some child care centers, you will have a one-on-one interview with the director or a staff member. In larger companies, you will start with the human resources department first. If you pass that interview, then you will be interviewed by the director or a member of the staff that you will work with at the center. Some companies like to conduct all of their interviews at once, so you would meet with a group.

The director and other staff members will interview you together.

To get a job at a child care center, you may also be asked to take a personality test. When this happens depends on the center. Some ask you to take this test before you come in for an interview. They use it as part of the screening process.

At some facilities, they may also ask you to work with the children as a part of the interview process. They want to see how you interact with the children. Just do what you know how to do.

Home Day Care Interviews

A home day care interview may take place before or after hours, or during the workday when there are children present. That is up to the owner. Ideally, you will be there when the center is up and running so that you can see what it is like day to day. While you are there talking to the owner, hopefully someone else will be taking care of the children. Otherwise, it will be a

A home day care interview will take place in the caregiver's home. Going there during working hours will help you see what the job is really like.

challenge to talk to someone who is taking care of so many little ones at once. You may be asked to come during their naps.

Caregiver-Child Ratios

While you are at the center for your interview, do a little math. Count the children and the caregivers. Does this center follow the rules?

The National Association for the Education of Young Children recommends one caregiver for every three to four babies, and no more than eight babies in a group. For ages two and three, it recommends one caregiver for every five to seven children. For the four- and five-year-olds, there should be one caregiver for every eight, nine, or ten children.

AN INTERVIEW WORKS BOTH WAYS

The person interviewing you wants to know more about you, but you need to make sure that it is a workplace that is good for you, too. Is it safe? Is it clean? Is there a regular daily routine (food, play, and nap) for the children? How many children will you care for at one time? What else will be expected of you?

The adults you will work with every day are also an important part of your job. How does the interviewer treat you? Could you work with this person day after day? Do you think the two of you will get along? What about the others who work there? Does the staff seem to work well together? Can you live and work with them day after day?

If the center doesn't follow these rules, it might not be the best place for you to work. Young children require a lot of hands-on care, and one person can only do so much. You don't want to get a job that is impossible.

Nanny Interviews

A nanny works for just one family, so you will be interviewed by one or both of the parents. Most families want to talk to you over the phone first. That will be your first interview. If you pass that test, you will be invited for a face-to-face interview in their home.

As a nanny, you will be a part of their family every day and will work without anyone supervising you. The interview will

When you are working as a nanny, you are the adult in charge. Before you start, find out how the family lives. What do they expect you to do?

be about who you are and what they want. You also need to find out how they live day to day. Here are some questions you can ask.

1. How does your family spend time together?
2. How do you discipline your child?
3. How do you want to communicate?
4. What do I need to know about your child's health and safety?
5. What will my duties be?

SMILE, YOU'RE ON CAMERA!

You may have seen news stories about nannies that were taken to court. One thing that is often mentioned in these cases is a nanny-cam. Yes, the families were watching their children and the nanny with a hidden camera. Video showing the nanny hurting the child was used as evidence in the trial.

Family members often want to see how you treat their child while they are away. This is the case whether you work in their home or at a child care center. In fact, some child care centers have cameras that film the children all day. Parents can log in to this private feed and see their children.

Wherever you work, never ever slap or spank a child in your care. If a child in your care is hurt, you could end up in court and in jail.

Never assume that you are completely alone with a child. Someone somewhere can record what you say and do. If there is not a camera in the room (hidden or not), there will be someone nearby with a cell phone. We live in a digital age.

After the Interview

As your interview ends, most employers will tell you what they are going to do next. Some will tell you that they are still interviewing other candidates. Others will simply say that they will be in touch.

When you get home after the interview, always follow up and send a written thank-you note. If the employer has been contacting you via e-mail, send a thank-you via e-mail. Otherwise, write a short note in a thank-you card and send it in the mail. A short handwritten note will make a good impression.

Don't stop looking for new jobs just because you had an interview. Keep looking at job boards and filling out job applications while you wait. Most employers will not contact you to tell you no. They will only call you back again if they are going to hire you. So don't sit around and wait to hear back. After a week has passed, you can call the office and ask if the job was filled.

CHAPTER FIVE

Your First Day at Work and Beyond

Your first day at work will be a time to meet new people and learn new routines. What those routines look like will depend on where you work. There are two forms that you must fill out

Your first day of work will start with paperwork. It's the same wherever you work. Your employer will want to know who your emergency contact is. Who will yours be?

wherever you work: a W-4 and an I-9. The W-4 is a tax form, and the I-9 is an employment eligibility form. Both of these forms are required by the federal government.

The federal government requires that employers send in taxes for all employees. Whenever you start a new job, you must fill out a W-4 tax form. This form tells the government how much tax you will pay during the year.

Remember to bring your Social Security number with you on your first day. You will need that number to fill out the W-4 form. It is proof of your identity as a taxpayer.

The W-4 form also has a worksheet on it. The worksheet will help you figure out how much tax your employer should withhold for you. The worksheet asks if you are single or married. It also asks if you are the head of a household or if you have any dependents. How much you will make and how many people at home you are responsible for will determine how much tax you pay. The wage charts at the bottom of the form will let you know how much tax your employer should withhold for you.

Before you go to work, visit the IRS W-4 Web page and figure out your taxes. Use the online IRS Withholding Calculator to make sure that you will be paying the correct amount. It has the same questions on it that the W-4 form does, but it asks only a few questions on each page. It also has links that pop up to explain the terms that the form uses. If you make a mistake, the Web page will tell you what to fix. It also allows you to go back, reset the page, or start over.

If your state also collects taxes, you will need to fill out a state form, too. The name of the form varies from state to state. In California it's DE 4, in Illinois it's IL W-4, and in Georgia it's G-4.

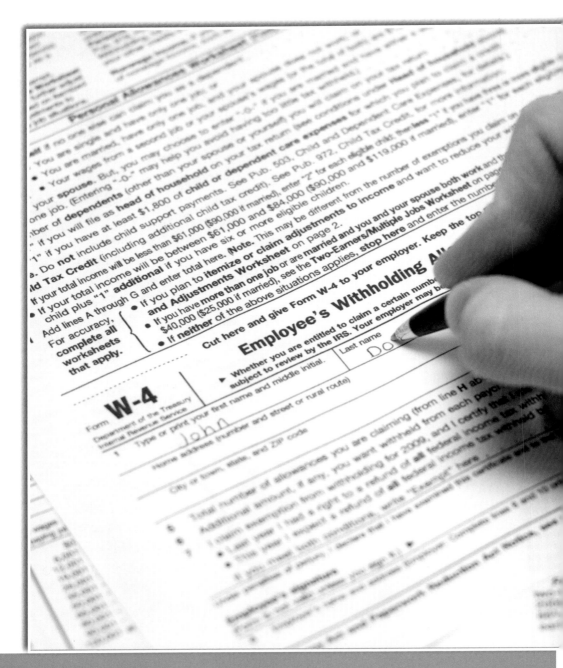

Before you start work, go to the IRS Web site and figure out your taxes. That will let you know what to write on your W-4 form.

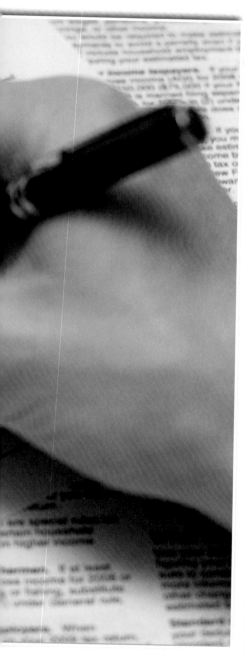

Another form that you must fill out wherever you work is the I-9. This is another form that the federal government requires for all new employees hired in the United States. Unlike the W-4 tax form, this form is not sent in to the federal government. It is to be kept on file at your employer's office for three years after you are hired. (If you change jobs, your old employer must save your I-9 for another year.)

The I-9 form will verify your legal status. It will also show that you are eligible to work in this country. You have to fill out this form even if you were born in the United States.

To complete the I-9 you must bring legal documents to show your new employer. These documents will verify your identity and your eligibility to work. For example, your driver's license verifies your identity and your Social Security card verifies your eligibility to work. You will need to bring both to fill out the I-9 form. If you have a U.S. passport, you need to show only that one document, and nothing else. A U.S. passport will verify both your identity and your eligibility to work.

These are the most common legal documents, but there are many others that you can use. Your employer is not allowed to tell you which documents are accepted. The I-9 form has a chart to show which ones you need. You can see a copy of the I-9 form online at the Department of Homeland Security.

Your First Day at a Child Care Center

On your first day at a child care center, you will probably not work with the children right away. You will spend time filling out your W-4 and I-9 forms as well as your emergency contact forms.

If the company has medical and dental insurance for their employees, you need to fill out these forms, too. Some of the larger companies also offer 401(k) programs. This is a special type of savings account for your retirement.

Your First Day at a Home Day Care

You will probably fill out a lot less paperwork at a home day care. The W-4 and the I-9 may be all of the paperwork you need. Insurance and retirement saving plans are not usually offered here. That doesn't mean that you don't need them. If the company you're working for doesn't offer them, you will need to look for them on your own.

Finding Health Insurance

No matter where you work, you need to have health insurance. If you work for a large company, it will have a health care plan for you. The only decision that you need to make is which type of plan you would like. On the other hand, if you're working for a very small company or for an individual, you will need to find your own insurance.

If you are under age twenty-six, you may be able to get insurance with your parents. If that is not going to work, you can get your own insurance. The government has a Web page

You can take care of your health insurance online. Every company has a Web site you can visit. After you sign up, you can go online to see your plan.

that can help you find a plan near you, so check online. Look at all the plans and see what works best for you.

Your First Day as a Nanny

Whether or not you fill out any paperwork on your first day as a nanny is up to your employer. Some families will do all of the paperwork needed to set themselves up as a legal employer. They will have you fill out the W-4 and the I-9. They will withhold income taxes from your paycheck. They will also pay your Social Security and Medicare taxes.

Another option that families use is a nanny payroll service. The families hire a payroll service to take care of your paycheck. You get paid, and the company does all of the paperwork. All of your taxes are collected for you, so you don't have to pay for the whole year in one big payment at the end of the year. It is easier to pay your taxes when the money is taken out in small amounts with each paycheck.

Some families do not want to handle any legal paperwork. They will just write you a check and let you take care of the rest. The family may tell you that you are a "contractor," so it is your responsibility to pay your own taxes. The IRS has lots of rules about the difference between an employee and a contractor. In fact, it has a twenty-page booklet titled *Household Employers Tax Guide* (IRS Publication 26).

A nanny is a caregiver with many responsibilities. How that works out can be different for each family. Make sure that you take care of yourself, too. Know what the law says about your situation.

According to the IRS, the difference between an employee and a contractor is who is in charge. When it comes to child care, there are three possible scenarios:

1) If you work as a nanny for a family in their home and follow their "specific instructions about household and child care duties," then you are their employee.

2) If you work for a nanny agency and the agency "controls what work is done and how it is done," then you are not the family's employee. The agency is your employer.

3) If you take care of the family's children at your home and you are in charge, then you are a contractor. You are your own employer.

You can't make the family follow the law, but you do need to know if they are breaking it. Some families don't want to pay any taxes. They don't want any records that show you work for them, either. They just want to pay you "under the table." Some will even pay you in cash so there isn't a paper trail. With cash there isn't any record of where the money went. All of this puts you in a difficult position. It's much better for you if everything is above board, if everything is legal, if everything is put into writing.

Nanny agencies recommend that the family create a written job description for you. Writing out a job description may seem like extra paperwork, but in the long run, it will protect you. It will put all of your duties in writing, and you can sign it and date it. Now everyone knows what is expected.

Most of the benefits offered by employers are not available to nannies. In 2012, *Forbes* magazine reported, "The nation-wide survey showed that less than a third of respondents were offered health insurance, less than half got two weeks paid vacation, and less than 3 percent received retirement plan contributions." If you work as a nanny, you will probably have to find your own health insurance. You will also need to set aside money from each paycheck for your retirement. How will you do that? Pay yourself first.

Pay Yourself First

Getting your first paycheck can be very exciting. After all this time, you finally have some money to hold in your hand. What will you do with it now?

Financial experts recommend that you pay yourself first. So what does that look like? Set aside 1 percent from each paycheck. If you make $100, put one of those dollars into a savings account.

It may not seem like much, but after a while it will add up. The more money you make, the more money you save. Having some money set aside will help you when you have an emergency.

Your goal is to save enough for you to live on for six months. How much money do you need to pay your bills each month? Multiply that number by six and you have your emergency fund goal.

On-the-Job Training

E xpect to learn more on the job after you are hired. You'll get to know the children and their parents better as each day goes by. You'll also develop deeper relationships with the other adults who work at the child care center.

Settling into a Daily Routine

Young children need a daily routine. It helps you and the child when everyone knows what will happen when. A center usually has a set routine that you need to follow. If you are a nanny, you will need to follow the children's old routine or start a new one for sleeping, eating, and playing.

Saying Hello and Good-Bye

Many children have a hard time when their parents leave them for the day. Some also have a hard time when their parents come back at the end of the workday. You will have to take care of both the parents' and the children's needs at these times. This is often the only time that parents are available to talk with you. At the same time it can be hard to talk with a clingy or crying child in your arms. This is when it can be very helpful to have a routine. The child knows that you

The children in your care will come and go every day. Having a routine for these times of change will help you and your families. Things go more smoothly when everyone knows what to expect.

will talk to Mom for just a few minutes. Then Mom will go to work in the morning, or they will both go home together.

Learning on the Job

As you adjust to the everyday routines, you will also learn more about the job itself. Some of this knowledge comes with practice. Some will come with training. In many states, you are required to take classes for a certain number of hours each year. Keeping up-to-date helps the children in your care. The children benefit from your knowledge and experience. The more you know, the better you can care for them.

The child care center may keep a list of new classes on the bulletin board in the break room. If you work at a smaller company, in a child care family setting, or as a nanny, you may need to find these classes yourself.

NATIONAL ASSOCIATION FOR THE EDUCATION OF YOUNG CHILDREN

The National Association for the Education of Young Children (NAEYC) is an organization you need to know. It has many resources for you, including national, state, and local learning programs that you can attend. At the end of each event you will be given a certificate of completion with "clock hours" that show how long the program was. Some NAEYC learning programs also count as continuing education units (CEUs). Which type you need (clock hours or CEUs) varies state by state, so look on your state's Web page to see what it requires.

Some job training classes are taught face-to-face while others are online. Before you spend any money on a training class, make sure that it is accredited in some way. Does your child care center accept the course work given by this program? Does the city or state accept it? You don't want to pay for a class that doesn't count.

Courses offered by universities often meet state child care training requirements. For example, if you live in Texas, you can take numerous online classes from Texas A&M. These classes count for both your state-mandated training requirements and your CDA. Some of these one-hour online courses are free. If you want to take the final exam and earn a certificate, you can do that for a small fee. For a one-hour class, the certificate fee is only seven dollars. The certificate fee for a two-hour class is twelve to fourteen dollars. For some courses even the certificate is free.

Paying for Your Training

Before you sign up for a class, ask your employer to pay for it. This is how it works with on-the-job training. If you need the knowledge for work, the employer will pay for the training.

Some companies set aside money for training each year. Even families with nannies may pay for training. If you can show your employers that the class will benefit them, they may pay all or part of the tuition. You won't know unless you ask.

New York has a MAT rebate program that will pay for your training every three years. These funds will be sent to your employer, so ask your employer to pay for the class.

If your employer wants you to pay for your classes first, make sure that you follow up. Make a copy of the certificate you earned and submit it with a printed copy of your payment. If the payroll department writes checks only once or twice a month, ask how long it will take to process. Write a note on your calendar so you remember. If a month passes and you haven't heard back, follow up and ask payroll about it.

You may be able to find a scholarship to pay for your training, too. If you have a scholarship, someone else pays the bills for your schooling. Your job is to go to class and learn. Most colleges have scholarship programs, but that's not the only place to look. Your state may have a scholarship program just for child care workers. You can find a list on the CDA scholarship page at the Council for Professional Recognition Web site.

For example, New York State has an Educational Incentive Program (EIP). An EIP scholarship pays for your college tuition and fees for early childhood education and

When you work in child care, you are the adult in charge. It is your job to help the children learn and grow. What you do matters. You are important!

training. This scholarship can also be used to pay for training outside of the college setting. If your training is required by the New York State Office of Children and Family Services regulations, the EIP scholarship covers it. You can use it to pay for your Red Cross training in first aid and CPR.

Day by Day

Day by day the time will go by, and soon you will have been working for an entire year. You're one year closer to earning your CDA certificate.

Your one-year anniversary is a good time to update your résumé. Add your current job to your work experience, and list your job title and the dates you have worked there (June 2013–present, for example). Then make a bullet-point list of five or six duties that you have. Maybe you "Read to children, and teach them simple painting, drawing, handicrafts, and songs."

After you update your résumé, think about what you want to do in the coming year. Will you "graduate" to a new position or stay where you are? Will the training you did during your first year at work help you get a raise? Will your employer help you pay for more training? What do you want to learn next? It's all up to you.

GLOSSARY

accredited Officially recognized as meeting the essential requirements.

administration The management of any office, business, or organization.

bureau A division of the government.

cardiopulmonary Referring to the heart and lungs.

certificate A document stating that a person has completed an educational course.

consumer A person who buys things.

credential Written proof of authority in a subject.

federal Referring to the government of the entire country.

grant A sum of money given to a person.

hygiene Personal cleanliness; clean or healthy practices.

immunization A shot given to protect a person from a disease.

license Formal permission from the government to do something.

nutrition Food; the study of how people eat.

psychology The science of the mind and human behavior.

résumé A brief written account of a person's qualifications and experience for a job.

resuscitation To revive, especially from apparent death or from unconsciousness.

statistics Numerical facts or data.

transcript An official school report of an individual student.

verify To prove the truth.

withholding Collecting taxes at the source of income.

American Red Cross National Headquarters
2025 E Street
Washington, DC 20006
(800) 733-2767
Web site: http://www.redcross.org/take-a-class
Get certified by taking two courses at the Red Cross: first
   aid and CPR for children and infants.

Canadian Child Care Federation (CCCF)
700 Industrial Avenue, Suite 600
Ottawa, ON K1G 0Y9
Canada
(800) 858-1412
Web site: http://www.cccf-fcsge.ca
The CCCF provides Canadians with early learning and child
   care knowledge and best practices.

Child Care Advocacy Association of Canada (CCAAC)
489 College Street, Suite 206
Toronto, ON M6G 1A5
Canada
(866) 878-3096
Web site: http://www.ccaac.ca
The Child Care Advocacy Association of Canada promotes a publicly funded, inclusive, quality, nonprofit
   child care system.

Childcare.gov
U.S. Department of Health and Human Services
Administration for Children and Families
370 L'Enfant Promenade SW

Washington, DC 20447

Web site: http://www.childcare.gov

A comprehensive online resource designed to link parents, child care providers, researchers, policymakers, and the general public with federal government–sponsored child care and early learning information and resources.

National Association for the Education of Young Children (NAEYC)

1313 L Street NW, Suite 500

Washington, DC 20005

(800) 424-2460

Web site: http://www.naeyc.org

Founded in 1926, NAEYC is the leading membership association for those working with and on behalf of children from birth through age eight.

National Network for Child Care (NNCC)

Iowa State University Extension

1094 LeBaron Hall

Ames, IA 50011

Web site: http://www.nncc.org

The NNCC is an Internet source of more than one thousand research-based and reviewed publications and resources related to child care with a newsletter and an e-mail forum for child care providers.

Office of Child Care

U.S. Department of Health and Human Services

Administration for Children and Families

370 L'Enfant Promenade SW
5th Floor East
Washington, DC 20447
(202) 690-6782
Web site: http://www.acf.hhs.gov/programs/occ
The Office of Child Care supports low-income working families through child care financial assistance and promotes children's learning by improving the quality of early care and education and after-school programs.

Web Sites

Due to the changing nature of Internet links, Rosen Publishing has developed an online list of Web sites related to the subject of this book. This site is updated regularly. Please use this link to access the list:

http://www.rosenlinks.com/JOBS/Child

American Academy of Pediatrics. *Caring for Your Baby and Young Child: Birth to Age 5.* 5th ed. New York, NY: Bantam Books, 2009.

Bray, Ilona, J.D. *Nannies & Au Pairs: Hiring In-Home Child Care.* Berkeley, CA: Nolo, 2010.

Brown, Harriet. *Babysitter's Business Kit.* Middleton, WI: American Girl, LLC, 2007.

Butler, Tamsen. *The Complete Guide to Personal Finance: For Teenagers and College Students.* Ocala, FL: Atlantic Publishing Group, Inc., 2010.

Chatzky, Jean. *Not Your Parents' Money Book: Making, Saving, and Spending Your Own Money.* New York, NY: Simon & Schuster Books, 2010.

Desrosiers, Alyce. *Nannies for Modern Moms: The Essential Guide for Hiring the Right Nanny for Your Child and You.* Sausalito, CA: Desrosiers and Associates, LLC Publishers, 2008.

Donovan, Sandy. *Budgeting Smarts: How to Set Goals, Save Money, Spend Wisely, and More.* Minneapolis, MN: Twenty-First Century Books, 2012.

Donovan, Sandy. *Job Smarts: How to Find Work or Start a Business, Manage Earnings, and More.* Minneapolis, MN: Twenty-First Century Books, 2012.

Hansen, Mark, and Kevin S. Ferber. *Success 101 for Teens: Dollars and Sense for a Winning Financial Life.* St. Paul, MN: Paragon House, 2012.

Hearron, Patricia F., and Verna Hildebrand. *Management of Child Development Centers.* 7th ed. Upper Saddle River, NJ: Prentice Hall, 2010.

Jana, Laura A., MD, FAAP, and Jennifer Shu, MD, FAAP. *Heading Home with Your Newborn: From Birth to*

Reality. Elk Grove Village, IL: American Academy of Pediatrics, 2011.

Kiyosaki, Robert T. *Rich Dad Poor Dad for Teens: The Secrets About Money—That You Don't Learn in School!* Scottsdale, AZ: Plata Publishing, 2012.

Macdonald, Cameron Lynne. *Shadow Mothers: Nannies, Au Pairs, and the Micropolitics of Mothering.* Berkeley, CA: University of California Press, 2011.

Musial, Tina. *How to Open & Operate a Financially Successful Child Care Service.* Ocala, FL: Atlantic Publishing Group, Inc., 2007.

Orman, Suze. *The Money Book for the Young, Fabulous & Broke.* New York, NY: Riverhead Trade, 2007.

Orman, Suze. *Women & Money: Owning the Power to Control Your Destiny.* New York, NY: Spiegel & Grau, 2010.

Sciarra, Dorothy June, et al. *Developing and Administering a Child Care and Education Program.* 8th ed. Belmont, CA: Wadsworth Publishing, 2013.

Segal, Marilyn, et al. *All About Child Care and Early Education: A Comprehensive Resource for Child Care Professionals.* 2nd ed. Upper Saddle River, NJ: Allyn & Bacon, 2012.

Thakor, Manisha, and Sharon Kedar. *On My Own Two Feet: A Modern Girl's Guide to Personal Finance.* Avon, MA: Adams Business, 2007.

Vermond, Kira. *The Secret Life of Money: A Kid's Guide to Cash.* Toronto, ON: Owlkids Books Inc., 2011.

Alexandria Technical and Community College. "Child Development Program Focus." Retrieved July 25, 2012 (http://www.alextech.edu/en/Students/Programs/Health/ChildDevelopment/ProgramFocus.aspx).

Best Résumé Samples. "Child Care Résumé Sample." Retrieved August 10, 2012 (http://www.bestsampleresume.com/resumes/care-taker/child-care-resume.html).

Bureau of Child Care NYC Department of Health and Mental Hygiene. "Types of Child Care." Retrieved August 13, 2012 (http://www.nyc.gov/html/doh/html/dc/dc-parents.shtml).

Carroll, S. L. "First Person: How Much Do I Need in My Emergency Fund?" Yahoo! Finance. Retrieved August 9, 2012 (http://finance.yahoo.com/news/first-person-much-emergency-fund-151100459--finance.html).

Childcarenet.org. "Earning Your Associate's Degree in Early Childhood Education (ECE)." Retrieved August 8, 2012 (http://www.childcarenet.org/providers/scholarships/ece/early-childhood-education-ece).

Collin College Child Development. "2012–2013 Child Development Program Information." Retrieved August 8, 2012 (http://www.collin.edu/academics/programs/childdevelopment.html).

Council for Professional Recognition. "High School Students Now Eligible for CDA." Retrieved August 10, 2012 (http://www.cdacouncil.org/announcements-and-events/156-hs-programs-now-eligible).

Covert, Bryce. "Nannies Making Six-figures? What Childcare Workers Really Take Home." *Forbes*, April 2, 2012. Retrieved June 4, 2012 (http://www.forbes.com/sites/bryce-covert/2012/04/02/nannies-making-six-figures-what-child care-workers-really-take-home).

Dragon, Debbie. "Pay Yourself First: What It Means, and How to Do It." Wisebread.com. Retrieved August 15, 2012 (http://www.wisebread.com/pay-yourself-first-what-it-means-and-how-to-do-it).

JobInterviewSite.com. "Child Care Résumé Sample." Retrieved August 10, 2012 (http://www.job-interview-site.com/child-care-resume-sample.html).

Lawyers.com. "Your New Job Comes with Paperwork." Retrieved August 9, 2012 (http://labor-employment-law.lawyers.com/human-resources-law/Your-New-Job-Comes-With-Paperwork.html).

McCombie, Sally M. "High School Child Development Courses Provide a Valuable Apprenticeship." Educational Resources Information Center. Retrieved July 25, 2012 (http://www.eric.ed.gov/ERICWebPortal/contentdelivery/servlet/ERICServlet?accno=EJ829516).

Nannies4hire.com. "Working with a Nanny Agency." Retrieved June 4, 2012 (http://www.nannies4hire.com/tips/1061-working-with-a-nanny-agency.htm).

NECPA Commission, Inc. "Certified Child Care Professional - (CCP): National Early Childhood Professional Program Accreditation." Retrieved August 8, 2012 (http://www.necpa.net/ccp.php).

Rose, Andrew G. "17 Tips to Ace Your Next Phone Interview." *U.S. News & World Report.* Retrieved June 10, 2012 (http://money.usnews.com/money/blogs/outside-voices-careers/2011/06/14/17-tips-to-ace-your-next-phone-interview).

Schulte, Brigid. "Secure in His Mannyhood." *Washington Post,* July 22, 2006. Retrieved July 18, 2012 (http://www.washingtonpost.com/wp-dyn/content/article/2006/07/21/AR2006072101686_pf.html).

U.S. Department of Labor, Bureau of Statistics. "Consumer Price Index: Frequently Asked Questions." Retrieved July 19, 2012 (http://www.bls.gov/cpi/cpifaq.htm#Question%2015).

U.S. Department of Labor, Bureau of Statistics. *Occupational Outlook Handbook*, 2012–13 Edition. Retrieved June 6, 2012 (http://www.bls.gov/ooh/personal-care-and-service/child care-workers.htm).

Vohwinkle, Jeremy. "Why You Need an Emergency Fund." About.com. Retrieved August 9, 2012 (http://financialplan.about.com/od/savingmoney/a/emergencyfund.htm).

Yoffe, Emily. "Diaper Genie." Slate.com. Retrieved July 23, 2012 (http://www.slate.com/articles/life/human_guinea_pig/2008/06/diaper_genie.html).

INDEX

H

Head Start, 20
health insurance, 6, 56, 57–58, 61
heatstroke, and children, 19–21
hidden cameras, 50
high school diplomas, 14, 21
home day care, 4, 5, 23, 28, 35, 46–48, 56

I

immunization records, 35
Infant/Toddler CDAs, 23
I-9 forms, 53, 55–56, 58

J

job applications, 28, 30–31, 35, 38, 42, 51
job boards, 31, 51
job fairs, 35–37
job search engines, 31, 34

L

legal documents, 53, 55–56, 58
licenses, 4, 35, 55
log, keeping a, 9, 12
Louisiana State Medical Society, 20

M

mannies, 6
Medicare, 58
medication administration training (MAT), 21, 65
minimum wage, 33–34

N

nannies, 4–5, 6, 12, 13, 28, 34–35, 40, 49–50, 58–61, 64, 65
National Association for the Education of Young Children, 48, 64
National Child Care Association, 21
National Highway Traffic Safety Administration, 19
networking, 37
New York State Office of Children and Family Services, 67
nutrition classes, 17

O

Occupational Outlook Handbook, 7

P

paying yourself first, 61
payroll services, 58
personality tests, 46
phone interviews, 38, 40–42, 49

Preschool CDAs, 23
preschools, 13, 14, 15, 20, 23
psychology classes, 17

R

Red Cross, 19, 42, 67
references, 30
résumés, 6, 28–30, 35, 43, 67

S

safety training, 17–19
salaries, 31, 33–34
scholarships, 24, 65, 67
Social Security, 53, 55, 58

student loans, 24
summer programs, 11

T

taxes, 6, 53–55, 56, 58, 60
thank-you notes, 51

U

U.S. Department of Labor, 33

W

W-4 forms, 53, 55, 56, 58

About the Author

Anastasia Suen is the author of more than 150 books for children and adults. She has worked in child care as a babysitter, a travel nanny, in family child care, in church child care, and in preschool child care. Suen has also taught kindergarten through college. She lives with her family in Plano, Texas.

Photo Credits